The fruit of the Spirit is the direct result of the life of Christ ministered to the believer by the Spirit . . . spiritual fruit is the outcome of the life of unbroken and full communion with Christ. "Abide in me, and I in you, so shall ye bring forth much fruit" (John 15). . . . Christ within us can accomplish what we can never hope to do in our own strength; and that continuous walking with Him will change the weakest of us into His image.— *taken from the book*

OTHER BOOKS BY DONALD GEE

Concerning Spiritual Gifts
Fruitful or Barren
God's Grace and Power for Today
God's Great Gift
Is It God?
A New Discovery
Now That You've Been Baptized in the Spirit
Spiritual Gifts in the Work of the Ministry Today
Temptations of the Spirit-filled Christ
This Is the Way
Toward Pentecostal Unity
A Word to the Wise

The Fruit of the Spirit

DONALD GEE

GOSPEL PUBLISHING HOUSE
SPRINGFIELD, MISSOURI
02-0501

12263506

Introduction

As mentioned in the opening chapter of this little book, the writer enjoyed the privilege of giving this series of Bible studies on the Fruit of the Spirit at the great annual Bible school of the Filadelfia church in Stockholm, probably the largest Pentecostal assembly in the world. It is in response to several kind requests that these addresses might be made available in a permanent form that this book has been written, from the notes of those lectures, during a voyage to South Africa.

The delightful theme of the Fruit of the Spirit, with all the various aspects of practical holiness pertaining to it, has inspired so many volumes from gifted writers that it seems almost impudence to add yet another, however unpretentious.

Yet there is one very attractive approach to this subject that still seems largely untouched; that is, the Fruit of the Spirit from a distinctly Pentecostal standpoint. It has been inevitable that a spiritual experience so powerful and crucial as that which the great Pentecostal Movement stands for should necessitate a revaluation of some previous experiences, and a revision of some previous doctrines. In this little book some small attempt is made in that direction; and the very important truths embodied in the subject of the Fruit of the Spirit are approached, expounded, and applied from the point of view of one definitely inside the Pentecostal Movement. Perhaps one slightly additional special feature is the frequent application of the subject to those engaged in the work of the ministry.

The student may be disposed to find fault with these studies, because they do not go thoroughly into the theological questions involved. The reason is, they have been purposely written for those faithful and beloved people who make up the bulk of our assemblies, and indeed of the Church Universal, and they therefore aim at being practical rather than theoretical. It is hoped that this feature will make them helpful to a far greater number than would be the case if they were mere attempts at bare theological studies. Keen students will have no difficulty in detecting the doctrinal views of the writer, as they are, of necessity, woven into the whole treatment of the subject.

But for the benefit of those specially interested in the theological side of the subject I may briefly say that I personally hold that doctrine of the Trinity necessarily implies that the work of the different Persons of the Godhead may be, and indeed must be, viewed from varying standpoints, each of which is correct as one side of truth, but does not contain all. Thus: we know that "God so loved the world that he gave his only begotten Son"; and yet, at the same time, and with equal truth, we know that "God was in Christ, reconciling the world to himself." In the same way, the Holy Spirit is sometimes viewed as the Spirit of the Father, or the Spirit of the Son, but on other occasions as a perfectly distinct Personality, separate from both.

The application of these sublime mysteries to the subject before us I suggest to be this: That these various Christian qualities of character listed as the "fruit of the Spirit" are the definite outcome of a new principle of life within a man, brought to him by the new birth "from above." The source of that life, and therefore the ultimate source of that "fruit" is Christ himself as an indwelling Saviour. The Scriptures plainly ascribe these things to Christ (Galatians 2:20; John 15:3; Philippians 1: 11, etc.). But this indwelling presence of Christ in the believer of necessity comes to him by the Holy Spirit, viewed in this respect therefore as the "Spirit of Christ," because the Son himself in His own proper personality, as the Second Person of the Trinity, is seated now at the Father's right hand on high. It follows that the "Spirit," who is the divine source of the "fruit of the Spirit," is the Holy Spirit specially considered in that one of His aspects described as the "Spirit of Christ."

The New Testament appears to record as an unmistakable historical fact that there can be, and should be, a separate personal reception by the believer of the Holy Spirit in His own distinctive and proper personality, subsequent to that first incoming at regeneration. This experience is called the "baptism in the Holy Spirit," and its purpose is not to impart life, but power. Its distinguishing manifestations are not fruit, but gifts.

This view certainly greatly helps to elucidate many of the practical difficulties that thoughtful and observant people encounter in these subjects. For it shows how it is possible for believers who have received the Spirit in regenerating power as the Spirit of Christ who dwells within them, to manifest much of His "fruit" without their ever receiving a definite experience of the baptism in the Holy Spirit. And on the other hand, it reveals how possible it is for believers to exercise certain gifts of the Spirit received through the Baptism, without showing forth the fruit of the Spirit—if they neglect to maintain the flow of the fullness of Christ's life within; in other words if they are not careful to "walk in the Spirit."

I know perfectly well that the above theological position is open to attack; but I would at least say this: The truth of the Triune Godhead surpasses human understanding to such an extent that, while we may feel justified in being dogmatic upon the central truth, we can be and ought to be very tolerant of one another's doctrines that are attempts to define the varying outworkings of it. Perhaps this is specially true of the Holy Spirit, for the exact definition of His person and work, being a part of the unsearchable mystery of Deity, represents a depth of theological truth that is worthy of much study and that only the light of the revelation can unfold.

And it is also respectfully submitted that a doctrine that appears satisfactorily to meet so many of the facts of experience has something to be said for its possibly containing vital truth. Nothing more than this is claimed. And with this I gladly leave the purely theological questions involved and turn to the increasingly congenial and, I think, more important practical side.

DONALD GEE

January 1934

Contents

The fruit of the Spirit is love, joy, peace, long-suffering, gentleness, goodness, faith, meekness, temperance (Galatians 5:22,23). *The fruits of righteousness, which are by Jesus Christ* (Philippians 1:11). *Abide in me, and I in you. As the branch cannot bear fruit of itself, except it abide in me* (John 15:4). *Wherefore by their fruits ye shall know them* (Matthew 7:20).

1

Fruit and Gifts

When I recently found myself faced with the privilege and responsibility of teaching once again in the great annual Bible school at Stockholm, I asked one of the local pastors if he had any suggestion to give me for a suitable theme. After a moment's pause he said, "The Fruit of the Spirit." I immediately saw the leading of the Spirit in the fitness of this; as it so perfectly balanced the studies "Concerning Spiritual Gifts"* given the year before.

The essential balance between these two themes must be obvious to all. Unfortunately there have admittedly been those who have laid considerable emphasis upon spiritual gifts, but seem to have sometimes neglected the fruit. Those who criticize them too hastily, however, will do well to remember that for generations past, and in many quarters at the present time, nearly all the emphasis has been laid upon fruit, and practically none upon gifts. Such an emphasis is equally unbalanced in the light of Scripture; and the pendulum always seeks to right itself.

*The author's book *Concerning Spiritual Gifts* is available from the Gospel Publishing House.

The New Testament is exquisite in its careful adjustment between the two subjects, both of which are integral parts of the working of the Holy Spirit. The 12th chapter of 1 Corinthians concludes a treatise on spiritual gifts with the significant words: "Covet earnestly the best gifts, and yet show I unto you a more excellent way." Thus the theme of love, a "fruit" of the Spirit, is introduced with a proper sense of proportion. Yet, lest the pendulum should swing too far the other way after such a brilliant hymn in praise of love as chapter 13, the 14th chapter begins with the equally significant words: "Follow after love, and desire spiritual gifts."

All through these three sane, eloquent, and practical chapters the balance is maintained. There is a strong insistence on the need of practical holiness for a profitable use of the gifts; but there is none of that almost brutal and fanatical opposition to spiritual gifts that seems to have marked some modern teachers on "Holiness."

Perhaps this perfect balance between "fruit" and "gifts" is also intentionally emphasized in the fact that there are *nine* of each, mentioned in the respective lists of Galatians 5:22,23 and 1 Corinthians 12:8-10.

Fruit Grows

The inspired choice of the term "fruit" is beautiful. Note the contrast between the "works" of the flesh and the "fruit" of the Spirit in Galatians 5. "Works" speak of the smoky city, noisy machinery, and feverish activity. "Fruit" speaks of the open countryside, the quiet of the garden, and the silent but life-giving forces of nature.

Fruit is the result of _life_. There is first the bud, then the blossom, finally the ripeness of harvest. Underlying all is the life in the tree itself that bears the fruit; also the life in the forces of nature, the sun, and the rain, that play upon it. Fruit is impossible where there is death.

The type is exact. The fruit of the Spirit is the direct result of the life of Christ ministered to the believer by the Spirit. "The fruits of righteousness which are by Jesus Christ" (Philippians 1:11). For spiritual fruit is the outcome of the life of unbroken and full communion with Christ. "Abide in me, and I in you, so shall ye bring forth much fruit" (John 15). Loss of communion is the explanation of most of our failure in spiritual fruit-bearing, and no amount of Christian work, or even exercise of spiritual gifts, can ever be a substitute for walking with God. It is encouraging to remember that sustained communion with Christ in our daily walk produces the fruit of the Spirit unconsciously. Others see it before we do. And it is better so.

This principle of unobtrusive growth provides a striking contrast to the way in which Christians can receive spiritual gifts. These are often (though not necessarily) bestowed on some special occasion, and with prayer or the laying on of hands, as in the Ephesian "Pentecost" (Acts 19:6), or when the presbyters laid their hands on Timothy (1 Timothy 4:14).

Many vainly seek the fruit of the Spirit in a wrong way. They go to camp meetings or conventions or to some special preacher, seeking the "blessing," and thinking that some fruit they specially desire, like peace or meekness, will be suddenly implanted within their nature there and then. Unless they walk with Christ they are doomed to disappointment.

I have told in a great many places an incident in my boyhood in London, when, one summer, I very much wanted to grow some tomatoes in our little garden. I bought my tomato plants, and carefully planted them and cared for them. But the smoky air of London did not help them very much, and by the end of summer I began to give up hopes of ever getting any fruit. Judge of my surprise, therefore, when one morning I saw some big ripe tomatoes hanging on my plants. I rushed to them with delighted amazement—only to find that my mother had tied them on with string! That simple joke of boyhood's days illustrates what many try to do with the fruit of the Spirit. They never fulfill the *conditions* for growing such fruit; and then try to make up for it by seeking an artificial method of production. But we can always see the "string"!

NOT BY THE BAPTISM

Many look to the baptism in the Holy Spirit as a means to produce the fruit of the Spirit, and express great disappointment if it is not immediately forthcoming after that experience. Yet the declared purpose and result of the Pentecostal Baptism is *power* for service and witnessing (Acts 1:8). Consistently with this purpose, the initial evidences of the Baptism are supernatural manifestations of the Spirit on the line of His gifts (Acts 2:4; 10:46; 19:6). Holiness is the evidence of a life of walking with Christ in unbroken communion, and may or may not have any immediate connection with a

14

Pentecostal Baptism. Much Christlike beauty of Christian character can exist apart from it.

On the other hand a genuine fullness of the Holy Spirit is bound to produce His fruit also, *because* of the quickened and enriched life of communion with Christ produced thereby. Nevertheless the immediate divine purpose at Pentecost was power, not holiness. Holiness by *faith* came before: and holiness by *obedience* had to follow after.

A babe in Christ can sometimes thus receive striking manifestations of the Spirit's power, accompanied by an obvious immaturity in the fruit of the Spirit which constitutes Christian character. This is plain in many of the early converts to Christianity to whom the letters of the New Testament were written. Genuine gifts of the Spirit of God can be exercised even where love is not perfected (1 Corinthians 13:1-3). Gifts apart from love are abnormal and in a believer of any maturity become inexcusable. Where love is absent the use of the gifts is reduced to utter worthlessness. Hence those who exercise spiritual gifts have the greatest need to show the fruit of the Spirit also; and to abide in "the apostles' doctrine" (Acts 2:42).

Fire and enthusiasm in public witnessing for Christ can ultimately defeat their own purpose if the life is not fragrant with the beauty of Jesus. We are all "living epistles, known and read of all men"; and the inconsistent life is the worst possible accompaniment to a great display of an apparent gift.

The Power of Fruit

This all goes to prove that there is a real power in the *fruit* of the Spirit. It is the quiet influence of a beautiful life, rather than the rushing power of a fiery ministry. And it comes from communion, and not from a crisis.

When the great Forth Bridge in Scotland was nearing completion we are told that one dull, cold day the builders tried unsuccessfully all day long to bring certain important girders together. Every available device of mechanical power was used, without success, and at the end of the day they retired completely baffled. But next morning the sun shone in summer warmth upon the great masses of steel, and the expansion thus produced soon enabled them to make the connection. So it is with much of the work of the Spirit: His power sometimes works more irresistibly in the silent influences of love, joy, and peace, than in the mightier manifestations of miracles or prophesying.

On the other hand there are often rocks that need blasting, and doors that need opening, for which the Pentecostal dynamite of spiritual gifts is an absolute essential. Philip found it so in his evangelistic work in Samaria (Acts 8:6), and Paul proved it in his missionary pioneering (Acts 13: 12; 14:3; 19:20).

The maximum manifestation of spiritual power is achieved only when fruit and gifts go together. In this connection the New Testament is careful to record that those who had outstanding spiritual power were not only men of gift but also men of grace and goodness (Acts 6:3; 11:24; 16:3; 22:12, etc.).

The greatest example of the principle that supreme spiritual power is found where supernatural gifts and spotless holiness of positive character meet together in perfect balance, is the Lord Jesus Christ himself.

16

2

Love

Love is undoubtedly the greatest of all the fruit of the Spirit. The first place given to it in the list of Galatians 5:22 is fitting and inevitable. For love seems almost to comprehend, when in perfection, all the fruit of the Spirit, and causes them to appear as so many phrases of its supreme glory.

To define perfect love—and the mature fruit of the Spirit is that—is a task beyond human tongue or pen. Paul comes very near it in 1 Corinthians 13, but then he was writing under the inspiration of the Spirit. God is Love, and therefore to try to define love is trying to define the Infinite.

One day, when in the Middle West of America, I tried to describe the Atlantic Ocean to an old lady who had never seen the sea in her life. I am sure I completely failed. Probably she received some sort of idea of a very big lake, but that was all. I always feel the same when I begin to talk about the love of the Spirit.

SOME CONTRASTS WITH NATURAL LOVE

But it is helpful to try a few contrasts; and es-

The Fruit of the Spirit Is Love

pecially to note those subtle but essential differences between purely natural love (which is *not* what the Bible means by the "fruit of the Spirit"), and truly spiritual love which is a direct result of our being made partakers of the divine nature by regeneration. Any thorough study of the fruit of the Spirit takes us clear down to the fundamentals of the New Birth. It is from the new life then received—the "law of the Spirit of life in Christ Jesus"—that all fruit of the Spirit grows.

It is to be remembered that the fruit of the Spirit is quite as truly supernatural as His gifts. It is not the result of improving the natural character; it is the result of a new spiritual life from above. Its possibilities are startling, gloriously so. It is within reach of the most unlikely in the natural; just as the gifts of the Spirit are bestowed upon those whom the world utterly despises.

(a) *Love for Enemies*

Natural love loves it own, flourishes in an atmosphere of friendship, and is fed by mutual manifestations of affection. Only on very rare occasions will natural love persist when no apparent return is given.

But the fruit of the Spirit goes beyond all this, for it even produces love for declared enemies. This is more than merely negative toleration; it is a positive activity moving us to do good to them who despitefully use us. It is one of the most remarkable features of Christ's gospel that He *commands* such a love (Matthew 5:46,47); and the very command implies, as always, the grace to fulfill it. That grace comes through the indwelling Spirit of Christ.

Our Lord himself was ever the most consummate exponent of His own teaching, and that type of love which is a fruit of the Spirit was most perfectly revealed when He prayed on Golgotha, "Father, forgive them, for they know not what they do."

As if to prove to the Church that it is truly possible for His Spirit to produce the same type of love in his followers, we have the example of Stephen, who prayed as his enemies stoned him to death, "Lord, lay not this sin to their charge." It was a living echo from Golgotha.

(b) *This Love Is Unchangeable*

One of the most common protestations of natural love is, "I will love you forever." Yet how often the passing years, and changing circumstances, see a cooling off. We declare the permanency of our love with all sincerity, and with much fervor too when young, but we know not our own hearts. For this reason advancing age sometimes tends to make men and women cynical where all love is concerned—unless they have discovered the secret of love as a fruit of the Eternal Spirit. Then there comes a revelation.

This element of unchangeableness in the love of Christ was wonderfully manifested in His love for Peter *after* his denial. Simon could have sung with rare appreciation, "Oh Love that wilt not let me go." Barnabas showed something of this fruit of the Spirit in the way he tenaciously clung to young Mark until that waverer became "profitable" (Acts 15:38; 2 Timothy 4:11). The same fruit of the Spirit today can often save a life, and sometimes a ministry.

(c) *It Is Also Sacrificial*

Natural love makes its nearest approach to the love of God at this point. For even natural love, when it is the real thing, proves its sterling character by a readiness to sacrifice for the one loved, sometimes even unto death. "Greater love hath no man than this, that a man lay down his life for his friends."

Yet divine love goes one better. "Peradventure for a righteous man some would even dare to die; but God commendeth his love towards us in that even while we were yet sinners Christ died for us" (Romans 5:7,8). Supreme love makes the supreme sacrifice, for those supremely unworthy. This seems the same as saying that divine love extends even to its enemies; but we specially mention it here because it is the very essence of the true spirit of Christian ministry. "The good shepherd giveth his life for the sheep" is not only written of Christ, but it ought to be true of every good shepherd of God's sheep.

Nothing is so necessary in a servant of Christ as this particular phase of the fruit of the Spirit. In many places the work of God languishes, not because of lack of gifts, but for lack of someone who will put a bit of really sacrificial *love* into it. A few gifts go a long way if mixed with much love.

One of the finest exhibitions of this fruit of the Spirit is the sacrificial love of a true missionary, exercised in naturally uncongenial places, and towards naturally unlovable people. Yet where there is real love the sacrifice is scarcely noticed, and *never* mentioned.

On one occasion my wife and I visited a Pentecostal mission station in a little Eastern town where the air was so foul that we were thankful to climb to the top of the hill for fresh air to overcome nausea. Yet that devoted missionary always referred to his location with genuine enthusiasm, and considered it one of the most beautiful spots on earth. Love transforms.

In pastoral work in the homelands there are many spiritual fathers and mothers with the sacrificial fruit of the Spirit who could say with Paul, "We were willing to have imparted to you, not the gospel of God only but also our own souls, because ye were dear unto us" (1 Thessalonians 2:8).

Sacrificial love in the natural can be foolish. The Spirit of God will make us not only sacrificial, but wise.

(d) Divine Love Is Sometimes Disciplinary

Natural love is never more prone to break down than when it deals with the duty of chastisement. Every spoiled child on earth is an illustration of this. "Whom the Lord loveth he chasteneth"; and fathers and mothers need the fruit of the Spirit to make them like God in this thing. The difficulty with most of us is to preserve the balance between anger and weakness. To chastise sincerely in love is a great accomplishment.

This is the crucial point in church discipline. There ought to be discipline in our assemblies (1 Corinthians 5:2); but to achieve its purpose of building up instead of casting down (2 Corinthians 13:10) it absolutely requires that divine love which comes only as a fruit of the Spirit. This is why some sincere attempts at church discipline have done more harm than good. They have lacked love.

Love given by the Holy Spirit rises above personal interests. One of its infallible marks is that it "rejoiceth in (or with) the truth" (1 Corinthians 13:6). The truth means more to it than all ties of natural affection.

We remember one sad instance where the son of a pastor had sinned morally in the assembly. The young man was unrepentant, and the plain duty of the pastor was to suspend him from membership until, like the prodigal, he "came to himself." But that pastor failed, and greatly injured the testimony for God in that place. It was an excruciatingly painful situation; we might any of us fail in the same way; but it reveals the necessity and provision made for us in the fruit of the Spirit. See how divine love insisted on the death of David's child, though it freely forgave the underlying sin (2 Samuel 12:14).

It has been said that "love is blind." This is true only of natural love. Spiritual love keeps its eyes very wide open to everything, acts accordingly—and keeps on loving!

The Bond of Perfectness

Paul expresses a beautiful ideal when he exhorts the Colossians to "above all things put on love, which is the bond of perfectness" (Colossians 3:14).

The passage always makes me think of the strong leather strap that I put around my suitcase for traveling. I throw all sorts of things into the case, some hard and some soft, some big and some small, some convenient to tuck in corners and some very awkward; but around them all and securing all together in a splendid unity is my big leather strap.

So it is with the church. We represent such a diversity of personality that often unity seems impossible; but the fruit of the Spirit which is the love of God can achieve it.

Sometimes we have thought that the gifts of the Spirit would inevitably bring unity. They undoubtedly would if they were always exercised in conjunction with the fruit of the Spirit. But the condition of the human spirit can so affect the manifestation and revelation of the Holy Spirit flowing through it, that even Christ can be preached in contention, and "tongues" can become "sounding brass." It is gifts and fruit working together in a sacred combination that alone will bring unity.

Thank God the final success is promised in His word. We shall "all come in the unity of the faith and of the knowledge of the Son of God, unto a perfect man, unto the measure of the stature of the fullness of Christ" (Ephesians 4:13). Spiritual gifts *exercised in love* always contribute towards that end.

When I first visited Stockholm in 1930 I saw the great new hall of the Filadelfia Assembly in process of erection. Everywhere workmen were busy, scaffolding surrounded the building, and noise abounded on every hand. Often since then, when I have looked over the finished and beautiful building, crowded with thousands of worshipers, I have been reminded of those frequently misinterpreted words at the close of 1 Corinthians 13. For in Stockholm it was the building that mattered, and was to be permanent, not the noise or the scaffolding. Yet the noise and the scaffolding were absolutely essential to the growth and completion of the building.

So it is with God's spiritual building in the church, and the illustration helps us to understand His purpose in spiritual gifts. It is the upbuilding of Christlikeness, as manifested in the *fruit* of the Spirit, that ultimately matters. But it is the purpose of spiritual gifts to help produce that eternal fruit. Some day the gifts will "pass away," *but not until their work is done.* And that day will arrive only when the final full manifestation of all the fruit of the Spirit is seen in all God's children when we meet our Lord. Then, shining above all, will be "the greatest of these—which is *love.*"

3
Joy

Everybody wants joy. Even those who deliberately choose a path of self-sacrifice that seems to make present joy naturally impossible, do so to obtain future and eternal joy. Christ himself endured the cross, and despised the shame, "for the joy that was set before him" (Hebrews 12:2).

NATURAL JOY

There is an entirely natural joy obtainable by entirely natural means. But it is *not* what is described as a "fruit of the Spirit"; for *that* is a result of receiving the Spirit, and walking in the Spirit.

Natural joy has certain characteristics that sharply distinguish it from spiritual joy (using the phrase "spiritual joy" here to denote the fruit of the Spirit). (a) In the first place, natural joy does not generally last, and has no elements of permanency (Ecclesiastes 7:6). Nothing illustrates this better than the feverish seeking by the worldly man for continual change and novelty in those means which he uses to promote his pleasure. (b) Natural joy always has a mysterious mixture of sorrow with it (Proverbs 14:13). The minor key persists in the music; there is a "skeleton at the feast"; a sense of insecurity pervades it. As a matter of fact a lot of apparent joy is a deliberate effort to drown care and willfully intoxicate the soul —"Let us eat and drink, for tomorrow we die." (c) Probably the purest form of natural joy is enjoyment of our *work*, and in many respects this is truly noble and satisfying. Solomon explored its possibilities to the full, and recommends it as the finest form of joy procurable "under the sun" (Ecclesiastes 2:10,11); but he also discovered final vanity, even here. Reasons for this are that the natural man knows that his grandest work must decay; the worker himself must some day leave it, often even before it is finished; and, even when consummated, human achievement often provokes jealousy and bitterness in others. These "flies" in the ointment of natural joy cause as much sorrow as satisfaction.

Jeremiah summed it up in his famous phrase of "broken cisterns that can hold no water" (2:13). The glorious message of the gospel is that God can give to men a joy that has none of these weaknesses, but is a "well of living water springing up unto everlasting life."

Not Cisterns But Wells

Spiritual joy is different in that it rises from a source that is pure. The heart that is right with God logically becomes capable of pure and eternal joy.

(a) The first joy which is a part of the fruit of the Spirit is therefore the joy of salvation—of sins forgiven. It consists in large measure of a sense of relief from an intolerable burden, or else the sense of a search rewarded and a hunger satisfied. In this class is the joy of the Philippian jailor, the Ethiopian eunuch, and the pearl merchant (Acts 16:34; 8:39; Matthew 13:46). Such a joy, though pure and eternal, is inclined to become selfish, and so this first phase of the fruit of the Spirit should ripen into—

(b) Joy in the salvation of others. Nothing so adds to real joy, and purifies it, as the sharing of the cause of the joy with somebody else. When the subject for joy is nothing less than salvation, the resultant joy found in sharing it is one of the fullest imaginable. Paul and Barnabas caused "great joy" to the assemblies when they told them of the conversion of the Gentiles (Acts 15:3). Those who have led even one individual to the Saviour know how deep is the joy involved. The same element enters into all that pure pleasure that redeemed children of God find in the progress of His work everywhere.

(c) Yet there is something deeper still. Joy in service is better than joy in merely personal blessing; but the ultimate joy in redemption is pure joy in God himself. Full-grown souls have found this all down the ages and in every section of the universal church. It is the ripe harvest of the fruit of the Spirit. Old Habakkuk has a remarkable passage in which he describes a scene of utter natural desolation, and then finishes with a triumphant burst: "Yet I will rejoice in the Lord, I will joy in the God of my salvation" (3:18). "Rejoice *in the Lord* alway," says Paul (Philippians 4:4). Such a joy becomes independent of outward circumstances, and even of inward blessings. It rejoices in a certain and sure possession of the *Blesser*. It is the essence of the eternal joy of heaven; it shares the present ecstasy of the glorified beings around the throne. The mountain-stream joy of personal salvation and then the broad river-stream of joy in service has broadened into the final joy of the limitless Ocean.

Because it is joy in God himself it is necessarily "everlasting joy" (Isaiah 35:10), for its cause can never fail. It is the final victorious answer to all the incompleteness of human and natural joy.

The Gardener at Work

Fruit comes to its best only by diligent cultivation, and the Master bestows much labor upon the ripening of the fruit of the Spirit in His people.

To establish the reality of their new joy in salvation from sin and to teach them to live alone in Him as their Fountain of joy, He often permits circumstances that are sharp enough to prove that no other causes for their joy continue to exist. Troubles come surging around, but the joy abides. The fruit of the Spirit is separate from outward circumstances. The classic example is that of Paul and Silas singing praises to God at midnight in prison, with their bodies aching from physical suffering, unjustly inflicted! It was a discovery worth making that they could *sing* in circumstances like that!

Christian joy often seems absolutely contradictory in the eyes of the natural man: "sorrowful yet always rejoicing" expresses it. Sometimes this joy of Christians even irritates those who know it not. "You ought *not* to be happy," was the indignant protest of a friend of mine on one occasion, when the irrepressible joy of salvation persisted in flowing over the lips in spite of genuine present sorrow.

But a still deeper lesson remains to be learned in that the Master will even withdraw ecstasy and joy in spiritual feelings in order to bring the soul to pure joy in himself. This is one of the lessons that come to those baptized in the Holy Spirit; and the process often puzzles them sorely at first, especially if no wise pastor or friend is at hand to give counsel and instruction.

A Lesson for Pentecostals

The initial stages of our Pentecostal experience usually contain much joy in the glory and happiness which they involve. This is the prime cause of speaking in tongues, because the exultation of our spirit can find no other means of expression. But there is the inevitable tendency to selfishly enjoy the spiritual excitement and transports of delight and to become introspective. The soul lives on its feelings, even those resulting from the fullness of the indwelling Spirit.

Consequently there will come sooner or later in the all-wise plan of God a time of testing, when the sensible *feelings* of the Holy Spirit's presence and power will be greatly diminished. This is to reestablish the unalterable principle of *faith* in the life that is to please God. The joy of the Spirit may seem to pass through a temporary cloud; but it is only that it may ultimately emerge as pure joy in God himself, independent of all feelings or manifestations, and happy in the certain knowledge of the assurance of faith that the Comforter has come to abide forever.

One of the cruelest mistakes we can ever make in the Spirit-filled life is to insist upon the outward signs of the joy in the form of continual manifestations, when the Lord is lovingly seeking to wean us from a selfish enjoyment of them for their own sakes. The mistake becomes deadly if manifestations become, first forced, and then finally imitated by the flesh. And, saddest of all, the desire of the heart never gets satisfied, for such travesties of genuine operations of the Holy Spirit cease to give the slightest joy whatsoever.

Unfortunately, not only individuals but assemblies make the same serious mistake. We have been in assemblies where the Holy Spirit was not working at the moment to produce emotional joy (the people likely stood in need of something else just then), but the saints themselves wanted to have all the old feelings of exhilaration; or else felt that their "testimony" demanded a semblance of it. Consequently one sees an attempt to work up an apparent joy which would be laughable were it not sad. Sometimes outward success seems realized, but the whole thing is entirely psychic and is a mere travesty of the true Pentecostal joy of the Spirit. Such joy springs up from within.

"My Joy ... in You"

Since all the fruit of the Spirit is the outcome of the life of Christ in the believer, it is noteworthy that He definitely promised His disciples that they should receive His own joy (John 15:11; 17:13). The component parts of this joy seem to have consisted in three main essentials:

(a) Joy in doing His Father's will (John 4:34).

(b) Joy in seeking "lost sheep" (Luke 15:5).

(c) Joy in His Father's wisdom and love (Luke 10:21).

30

We can easily see how these three sources of our Lord's earthly joy correspond with the three phases of our own joy as a fruit of His Spirit in our lives that we have already studied:

(a) Our first joy in deliverance from sin. Christ had no sin; but sin is essentially rebellion against the known will of God; and our first steps of willingly and gladly doing God's will marked our first real deliverance from the guilt and power of sin and linked us with the pure joy of Christ's perfect obedience to His Father in everything.

(b) Our joy in service, and in sharing in His great task of seeking and finding the lost; and "sharing the travail that makes thy kingdom come."

(c) Our ultimate and fullest joy when we receive the revelation of the wisdom and love of God to our own souls by the Spirit, and love Him for himself.

4

Peace

Last night I sat on the deck of an ocean liner, looking up at the stars, while the vessel was steadily streaming through calm waters, on a cool night in the tropics. In the chair next to me was a fellow preacher, and we were enjoying conversation about the things of God. All day long the decks had been the scene of ceaseless activity and busy games among the passengers; and that just seems to typify the contrast that one often feels between peace and joy. There come times to every one of us when we long for peace even more than ecstasy. One of the most beautiful names given to our Father in heaven is "the God of peace" (Romans 16:20; 2 Corinthians 13:11). Perhaps the most satisfying benediction that we can ever pronounce is "The peace of God that passeth all understanding keep your hearts and minds. . . ."

A WONDERFUL LEGACY

We usually like to arrange for our most treasured possessions to go to those we love the most.

The Fruit of the Spirit Is Peace

It seems as if some desire like that was filling the heart of the Lord Jesus the same night that He was betrayed. "Peace I leave with you, my peace I give unto you," He said to His disciples (John 14:27).

How wonderful His peace had always been! In the storm on the lake He knew no agitation; before demons He was utterly master of the situation; as for the hostile crowd, He simply passed through it, defended by a tranquillity that was invincible. John Wesley testifies in his *Journals* to something of the same kind of peace when he faced the mobs of his day: it was the fruit of the Spirit, his personal share of Christ's great legacy to all His true servants.

There is a fine story of an old martyr who, as the fire was being lit around him, asked the officer in charge to place his hand over his heart. Its perfect quietness so amazed the persecutor, that he, too, became a Christian.

This peace, this divine legacy from our Saviour, is brought into our hearts and lives as a fruit of His indwelling Spirit.

PEACE SOMETHING THAT GROWS

Of course it begins for us in the place where His peace always had rested from the beginning—in being absolutely *at one with* the Father. Its only true source in our lives is in the atonement. "Therefore being justified by faith, we have peace with God through our Lord Jesus Christ" (Romans 5:1). It is "peace through the blood of his cross (Colossians 1:20).

This is the beginning: but peace can and should grow. On Nov. 11, 1918, the Armistice caused the guns to be silent, and peace took the place of war. But the nations had been organized for war, and it took very many months for actual conditions of peace to spread over all the lands. Great ammunition factories had to be transformed or scrapped; and millions of soldiers had to be demobilized and gradually drafted back into peaceful occupations.

So it is with the soul: conversion means the laying down of the arms of rebellion and warfare with God, but there is often quite a time before the whole being comes under the benign influence of His peace. With many Christians such a peace never extends beyond a sense of sins forgiven, and an assurance of pardon at the last. Their personal lives are marked by fretfulness and anxiety; and even in the church they are a frequent source of disturbance and restlessness, having very little peace themselves and disturbing the tranquillity of others.

THE BATTLEGROUND OF THE MIND

It is in the mind that the fiercest battles usually rage. This gives an added beauty and significance to those lovely words in Isaiah 26:3: "Thou wilt keep him in perfect peace whose mind is stayed on thee." It is the picture of a mind at rest because it is filled with a knowledge of the Almighty, and knows that He is enough for every situation. Such peace is truly a fruit of the Spirit, for it is His work to enlighten the eyes of our understanding to know God in Christ (Ephesians 1:17,18).

We sometimes forget that we can fill our minds with whatever we choose. So many seem to regard the mind as a helpless victim of circumstance all the time; but this is not true. Paul has a famous passage in Romans 8:6, where he says, literally, "The mind of the flesh is death, but the mind of the Spirit is life and peace." Perhaps we

34

could render it "the minding." Moffatt translates it, "The interests of the flesh mean death, but the interests of the Spirit mean life and peace." In any case the teaching is quite plain. If we want peace we must have our interests in the things of the Spirit. We can deliberately choose to fill our minds with these things—by company, by habits, by books, by meetings, by meditation, and by work for Christ. If we let our minds become filled with worldly things we must not be surprised if we lose the peace of God. A man might as well complain at having bad dreams at night if he reads an exciting criminal story before going to bed!

There are two very specific means by which our minds can be kept in the peace of God. (a) The first is by taking everything to God in *prayer with thanksgiving.* "Be anxious for nothing; but in every thing by prayer and supplication with thanksgiving let your requests be made known unto God; and the peace of God which surpasseth all understanding shall keep as with a garrison your hearts and minds in Christ Jesus" (Philippians 4: 6,7, Newberry). (b) The second is by loving in a practical way the Word of God. "Great peace have they which love thy law: and nothing shall offend them" (Psalm 119:165). Daniel is often considered to have been the author of the 119th Psalm; and if that is so, we have here a revelation of the source of that peace he enjoyed even when in the lions' den. What a contrast he offered to the poor, sleepless king! (Daniel 6:18).

Those who observe these rules will surely find the fruit of the Spirit, which is peace, growing in their hearts. And what a blessing they will, often quite unconsciously, be to others!

35

But the peace of God is not only a personal blessing for each individual child of God: it is a heritage for our united life in the church. "The peace of God . . . to the which also ye are called *in one body*" (Colossians 3:15). Assemblies without peace are indeed wretched places.

The fact that peace is our united inheritance in Christ does not do away with the fact that we have to guard it carefully. One special way to do this is to avoid all needless controversy—"Foolish and unlearned questions avoid, knowing that they do gender strife" (2 Timothy 2:23). Some personalities simply love argument for its own sake. And some foolish people do not seem to know when, where, or how to keep their mouths shut on a controversial subject. But happily some do.

When I was in Australia I had told to me a beautiful incident illustrating this point. A certain British preacher had been giving teaching on some nonessential doctrine with which the Australian assemblies did not agree. Very nervously a young pastor, with his deacons, approached him on the subject and asked him to desist for the sake of the peace of the assembly. The famous evangelist looked fierce for a moment, and said, "Do you know what I am going to do?" They said "No"; and thought that perhaps he was going to terminate the special meetings immediately. (Some would)! To their delight he replied, "I'm going to give you a kiss all around." He did; and never mentioned the debatable subject again. Oh, for more men of such wisdom and grace!

Another subject specially to watch for the preservation of peace in Pentecostal assemblies is the use of spiritual gifts. Rightly exercised in the Spirit, these should always minister peace and concord. Paul sums the matter up with the words, "God is not the author of confusion but of peace, as in all churches of the saints" (1 Corinthians 14:33). Some of the uses they were making of the gifts of the Spirit at Corinth were not adding to the harmony of the assembly there; but that was because the "spirits of the prophets" had got a little out of hand. If we want the vital fruit of peace to grow in our assemblies we must watch this point very carefully. It is not saying too much to affirm that as a general rule we can test the degree to which the exercise of a gift is in the Spirit by the way in which it either hinders or helps the peace of the assembly—always presuming that the assembly is one that sincerely wants the Spirit of God to have His way.

Assemblies that enjoy spiritual rest are always the healthiest; and consequently the development of this fruit of the Spirit is one of the surest preparations for increase in every way. "Then had the churches rest (peace) . . . and were multiplied" (Acts 9:31). True peace is not a synonym for laziness; it provides the necessary background for all happy and profitable activity. It is the essential atmosphere of the busy harvest field.

5

Longsuffering

Long-suffering takes us right back into the beginnings; when the history of God's dealings with men was young. "When once the long-suffering of God waited in the days of Noah" (1 Peter 3:20).

But it is rather remarkable that the circle is complete, and it is again the long-suffering of God that operates in the end, holding back the inevitable day of doom as long as possible. "The Lord is not slack concerning his promise, as some men count slackness; but is long-suffering to us-ward, not willing that any should perish, but that all should come to repentance. But the day of the Lord will come . . ." (2 Peter 3:9,10).

AN ATTRIBUTE OF GOD

Long-suffering, which is a fruit of the Spirit, is one of the attributes of the Almighty. It forms part of the eternal *name* (Exodus 34:6), and is one of the most frequent reasons given for worship and praise.

Its special revelation occurs in the divine patience and mercy toward sinners (not toward their

The Fruit of the Spirit Is Long-suffering

sin). This gracious attribute of the Godhead takes on an even brighter luster when we remember that all sin ultimately represents a personal offense against a personal God. It is the consciousness of that that causes those who have become reconciled to God through Christ to appreciate His long-suffering in a very deep way. Paul said, "For this cause, I obtained mercy, that in me first Jesus Christ might show forth all long-suffering for a pattern" (1 Timothy 1:16).

The purpose of divine long-suffering is to bring men to repentance (Romans 2:4). It is important to remember this: it is patience with a purpose. God's long-suffering is very strong and purposeful. It is not a mere passive endurance that has no particular end in view. In this it differs from mere resignation to the inevitable.

Because of this it follows that true long-suffering is an essentially voluntary thing. God does not have to suffer long with offenders. He does it because "love suffereth long and is kind" (1 Corinthians 13:4); and those who show long-suffering do it with a strong purpose of kindness.

A Fruit of the Spirit

It is worth considering long-suffering at its source in the heart of God, when we remember that this fruit of the Spirit is the direct result of our being made "partakers of the divine nature," and that it only grows into maturity as we live in communion with God.

The likeness between God and His children can become very beautiful in this thing. I shall never forget a chance remark I heard dropped by a faithful pastor when I was a very young man. Some of us were marveling at the way he bore with the insults and perversity of certain people who were bitterly opposing him, and seeking to hinder and injure his ministry by every means in their power. "God bears with them, and therefore so can I," was all he said.

There is a noteworthy statement concerning long-suffering in Colossians 1:11: "Strengthened with all might, according to his glorious power, unto all patience and long-suffering with joyfulness." Two things are specially striking about this passage: (a) That the purpose of such a divine enduement of power should be long-suffering. We usually think of the bestowal of might and power as for the one specific purpose of performing mighty works in His name, and conducting a powerful and gifted ministry. Yet here the declared end of power is "long-suffering." This may give a new light to some people on the purpose of the baptism in the Holy Spirit. It is surely sometimes bestowed to make men "pillars" in the church (Galatians 2:9), and such men are always of supreme value and importance. Some brilliantly gifted preachers and busy workers for Christ have little value as "pillars," simply because they do not exercise sufficient long-suffering. Yet their own ministry would have little opportunity for exercise if it were not for the established assemblies that exist only because of pastors and elders who are veritable pillars.

(b) The second noteworthy thing in this passage is that it is to be "long-suffering *with joyfulness*." Now this is important, because there are some people who cultivate a certain caricature of true long-suffering. They boast of their patience, and never cease to advertise their own remarkable resignation and meekness. Their sighs would do credit to a steam engine! All this is not the fruit of the Spirit: the long-suffering He gives is a happy thing—it sings. Moffatt translates the passage "to be patient cheerfully."

The Product of God's Winters

When I left my home in England recently it was in the depth of winter; many trees were leafless and frost was on the ground. I walked around the flower beds in the garden and thought of the gay-colored blossoms that had filled them last summer: all had fled now. It was only in the greenhouse that we were able to prepare seedbeds for an entirely fresh crop of the delicate annuals. Yet outside were grand, sturdy old trees as full of life as ever, their roots deep down in the warm soil; and clumps of hardy perennials were already pushing their heads through the ground to see if spring were on the way.

Long-suffering has the characteristics of those grand old trees just because it is the product of God's winters, as well as His summers. It has the strength of all things that attain maturity only through trial. It is obviously a fruit of the Spirit which is impossible without testings. For who can "suffer" at all without hardhip? And who can learn to suffer "long" without a sustained ordeal? Surely the divine purpose in many of the trials of God's children is to produce and perfect in the only way possible this fruit of the Spirit.

Trouble can affect a man in one of two opposite ways. It can either make him bitter, or make him tender. Job and Joseph are the two great examples in the Bible of tribulation working patience; and it is one of the loveliest things in history to see

41

Joseph, after ten years in prison through gross injustice, emerging as sunny and free from bitterness as a spring morning, with faith undimmed and love triumphant.

THE SIGN OF AN APPROVED MINISTER

True long-suffering is rather a rare thing. We frequently find its ugly opposite, which is hastiness and short temper. And, let us whisper it very quietly, sometimes even preachers do not show as much long-suffering as they ought.

The Bible itself has some examples. There was Jonah, for instance, who could preach a great city into repentance, but was as bad-tempered as could be about the gourd (Jonah 4:9). We are afraid he was not the last fiery preacher of judgment who could be exceedingly irritable, when out of the pul-may succeed as prophets and evangelists; but they make very poor pastors!

Even the twelve apostles provide an illustration of impatience in their treatment and hasty dismissal of the women who brought their little ones to Jesus. There are some types of spirituality which *do* always seem strangely impatient with children. But the Lord Jesus was not like that.

No man can afford to neglect the fruit of the Spirit which is long-suffering if he wants to become an approved minister of God. The Scripture definitely includes it among the necessary marks of such a man (2 Corinthians 6:4-6).

He must remember to manifest it in his preaching. We have to "reprove, rebuke, exhort with all long-suffering and doctrine" (2 Timothy 4:2). Nothing is easier than to let a note of impatience and irritability creep into our sermons. Sometimes the pit, if things did not go all his own way. Such men

42

people seem so slow to understand, and so slow to evidence any appreciation. It takes the Spirit of Christ to be willing to repeat the same truths over and over again, in the simplest language we can find, until at last the people really do begin to seem to take it in. Whether they understand the doctrine or not, the preacher may be perfectly sure that they feel what manner of spirit he is of; and nothing will so effectually close their hearts against him as a feeling that he is impatient with them. I remember on one occasion, at a convention in England, when a speaker actually chided the congregation from the pulpit for their inattention. And he was speaking about Calvary to a company of believers! Poor preacher: no wonder we heard very little more about him. He needed to look within for the reason of his failure. It was sheer head knowledge; and he became impatient because we refused to be dazzled while our hearts were unmoved.

Lives preach louder sermons than words, and so a preacher's "manner of life" must show forth all "long-suffering" (2 Timothy 3:10) if he is to win souls. I have sometimes been amazed at the way some of the most active pastors I know, men in charge of large and busy assemblies, seem to have unlimited time and patience to talk with, and visit, all sorts of often unreasonable and apparently unimportant people. But is this the secret, after all, of their success? I think it is.

6

Gentleness

At a certain steelworks in England they have a very powerful steam hammer. After explaining and displaying to visitors its exceptional power, the demonstrator usually finishes with the use of this great hammer to crack a nut! And the nut is cracked as gently and as neatly as with a small pair of hand crackers. *That* is true gentleness.

For gentleness must never be confused with mere weakness. Gentleness is power under perfect control.

THE GENTLENESS OF GOD

It takes part of the rugged strength of manhood and part of the controlled tenderness of womanhood to make the very finest gentleness. It is kindness in the very best and fullest sense of the word.

For God is gentle; and to manifest gentleness as a fruit of the Spirit is truly to be like God in one of the best-beloved of His attributes. "Ye shall be the children of the Highest; for he is kind" (Luke 6:35).

The Fruit of the Spirit Is Gentleness

When men, under the inspiration of the Spirit, want to describe this particular characteristic of the Almighty they usually speak of Him as a "Shepherd." It was this gentleness that made David not only great (Psalm 18:35), but led him to commence the best loved of all his psalms with the words, "The Lord is my shepherd." The loving-kindness of the Lord is a constant theme of praise.

Perhaps the passage that helps us to understand and appreciate divine gentleness best of all is Isaiah 40:10-12. The central verse is full of quiet, strong beauty: "He shall feed his flock like a shepherd; he shall gather the lambs with his arm, and carry them in his bosom, and shall gently lead those that are with young." Yet the verses immediately before and after this gem of exquisitely revealed gentleness contain eloquent descriptions of both the power of the arm of the Almighty Ruler and His infinite wisdom as the Creator of the ends of the earth who has meted out heaven with a span. This is superb contrast. And it gives a correct conception of true gentleness—power, under the control of perfect love.

Paul speaks in one place of "the meekness and gentleness of Christ" (2 Corinthians 10:1). In Him was fulfilled the prophecy, "A bruised reed shall he not break, and the smoking flax shall he not quench" (Isaiah 42:3).

The gentleness of our Lord was manifested in His dealings with the sick, the poor, the young, and the fallen. All who were among life's "broken reeds" felt its kindness. There is a beautiful touch of gentleness when He raised the daughter of Jairus from the dead. First He puts outside all the noisy mourners and takes the father and mother in alone; then in an exquisitely gentle way He takes the hand of the maid, and awakens her from the sleep of death; lastly, there is a final touch in the command to give her some food.

It is true that He sometimes rebuked fevers, and was stern with demons; but we have sometimes thought that those who now act in His Name *could* be a little more like Him in gentleness at times.

GENTLENESS WITH SOULS

Gentleness is a fruit of the Spirit of God which is of first importance in a minister of the gospel, because his work is often of such a delicate nature. The human soul is the most wonderful thing God ever made, and to handle it in any vital way whatsoever (as a minister is often and properly called to do) requires a skill imparted by heaven itself, and kept to perfection by a close walk with God.

Those of us who are not set apart for the special work of the ministry do well to remember that we all have much to do with one another's souls as we go along life's pathway. We all need gentleness to keep us from inflicting needless injury, and to give the touch of help so often needed.

(a) *As a Mother with Children*

Paul, in writing to the Thessalonians says, "We were gentle among you, even as a nurse cherisheth her children" (1 Thessalonians 2:7). We have to remember that beginners in the Christian life are described by the Spirit as "newborn babes" (1 Peter 2:2).

Older believers sometimes seem to forget this. They set unreasonable standards for young converts that are only applicable to Christians of ripe experience. We do not for one moment suggest that ultimate standards of holiness should be or need to be altered; but we do believe there is room for much gentleness and kindness while new believers grow in grace. Mothers and nurses are very gentle with little children who do not yet know how to behave at the family table; and certainly do not scold the toddler who falls down a few times while taking his first steps. We need a few more Elishas to tell Naamans to "go in peace" instead of loading them with burdens too heavy to be borne (2 Kings 5:18,19). Lack of reasonable gentleness has sent some promising converts back into the world.

When a believer recently baptized in the Holy Spirit makes some mistake in the use of a spiritual gift in the public assembly it is downright brutal to correct such a one in the public meeting. If it simply must be done then the utmost gentleness and tact should be used. But private admonition should always be the way preferred by true kindness.

In the same way, it is really a lack of true kindness to hurry any young believer into office. No wise mother or nurse would act so with her charges. "Not a novice, lest being lifted up with pride. . ." (1 Timothy 3:6). We pay dearly for our mistakes afterwards.

Babes have to receive "the sincere milk of the word," but it takes gentleness to feed them skillfully, as anyone who has had to feed a natural baby with a bottle knows very well. Some pastors (and some Sunday school teachers!) have yet to learn the art of conveying the word in the form of "milk." Don't complain when your charges lose their spiritual appetite if you feed them on the tough meat of systematic theology suitable for third-year students in a seminary; or on the bones of some controversial doctrine best discussed only at a private presbytery meeting! Have you ever thought that this is unkind?

(b) *As a Nurse with the Sick*

Could anything exhibit gentleness and kindness more perfectly than the way of a skillful nurse with her patient? And, unhappily, many people fall sick in soul.

We know the usual symptoms; and how strikingly analagous they are in the physical to the spiritual realms! Loss of appetite, irritability, supersensitiveness, quickness to take offense, peevishness, nothing pleases, a dislike for work, a moping desire to keep away from the rest of the family. All these are infallible marks of the sick Christian.

There certainly is a temptation to get angry with folk in such a condition, and we feel that a good shaking, and some rough words, might do them a lot of good. But usually gentleness pays better. "The servant of the Lord . . . must be gentle unto all men, apt to teach, patient, in meekness instructing those who oppose themselves" (2 Timothy 2:24,25). Many a pastor has won some of his most loyal members through persistent gentleness, in the face of irritability and willful misunderstanding.

Sometimes when people are sick we have to keep the room very quiet, and cannot allow ourselves to whistle or sing or engage in a lot of talking, however much we who are full of health feel like it. Now we are not going to advocate anything approaching quenching the Spirit; but we *do* suggest that His gentleness will move us to control

48

some of the exuberance of our own feelings on many occasions when we know that we are in the presence of believers not so full of life and health as we are spiritually. This is only conforming to the scriptural principle of not letting our personal liberty become a stumbling block to a weaker brother. And the gifts of the Spirit will never conflict with the fruit of the Spirit when exercised "in the Spirit."

(c) *As a Craftsman with His Work*

One day I watched a potter at work with his wheel. The thing that impressed me was the marvelous sensitiveness of his fingers, and the permanent form given to the vessel by the slightest touch of pressure upon the clay. There is always something instructive and ennobling in skilled craftsmanship.

God's craftsmen need the most skilled touch of all; their work is of such eternal importance. Part of that skill that is highly necessary for such master-craftsmanship is gentleness. James includes it under wisdom, and tells us that, "The wisdom that is from above is first pure, then peaceable, gentle and easy to be entreated, full of mercy . . ." (James 3:17). All this, when directed in blessing upon other souls, brings the touch of an expert. And there is always room for experts.

What skilled gentleness is needed in winning souls! It is instructive to watch the Master at work, with Nathaniel, with Nicodemus, with the woman at the well, with Zaccheus, with Peter. Yes, and with you and me. Thank God that He has many experts still today, who are highly skilled and equipped with the fruit of the Spirit, which is gentleness, for this greatest of all tasks.

There is needed the skill of a really good pilot in the assembly—the man who can provide "Holy Ghost chairmanship," and keep the whole meeting off the rocks, and in the deep water of the fullness of spiritual blessing, with a minimum of flurry and self-assertiveness. Of course such a brother, if he is a real expert, will have the spiritual gift and office of "governments" (1 Corinthians 12:28; literally, "pilotage"). But we are certain that accompanying his gift will be the fruit of gentleness.

On rare occasions, in a great vessel steaming full speed ahead at sea, an emergency will compel a sudden alteration in the ship's course. But it nearly shakes the vessel to pieces, and strains every part. It is the practice of a pilot to steer the ship gently, and only the greatest emergency alters this rule. What a jar it brings to an assembly or a convention when the chairman acts arbitrarily or without gentleness.

What a contrast is provided by the superb gentleness with which a giant liner is always brought into dock. The vessel is slowed down until it scarcely seems to be moving, quite silently it draws closer and closer to the shore, a thin line is thrown, then a thicker, and so, yard by yard the huge boat is brought safely against the pier.

I was even more impressed by the landing of a big airplane, for I really did expect a bump then, and we had been warned to strap ourselves to the seats in case of such an eventuality. Yet the pilot brought the big machine down so skillfully that we landed with hardly a perceptible jolt. The Lord wants pilots in His assemblies who can do things like that with a meeting.

In the completion of the eternal purpose of God in pouring out His Spirit in power at Pentecost, there will always remain an essential place for the fruit of the Spirit which is gentleness. It is one of the most necessary accompaniments of great spiritual gifts, and marks the worker who has the enduement of power from on high under the control of perfect love.

7
Goodness

Goodness is something that has fallen into a kind of disrepute these days; not, indeed, the actual quality, so much as the word that describes it. In England we sometimes call certain people "goody-goody," by which we mean a type that is sickly sanctimonious, with often a taint of hypocrisy about it.

In modern usage the word that best seems to denote that true, robust goodness which is a fruit of the Spirit is the word "sound." Thus we often speak of merchandise as sound goods; we speak of a cobbler as making a sound job of repairing our shoes: and we expressively describe certain people as sound people.

By such a phrase we do not usually imply any special cleverness—rather the reverse. By *sound* people we intend to convey the thought of qualities of character, rather than of gift. What we particularly have in mind is that they have a well-proportioned personality, are dependable, have a thoroughly honest character, and make excellent

---

The Fruit of the Spirit Is Goodness

company in all the ordinary walks of life. This is true "goodness." And a very fine thing it is too!

PASSIVE GOODNESS

There seem to be two sides to goodness. Perhaps we might term them *passive* and *active;* though passive here can only be used in a strictly relative sense, for it is used of something very actively influential.

Our Lord described passive goodness when He likened His disciples to the "salt of the earth" (Matthew 5:13). The thought is plainly of that unseen, silent preservative effect that salt has upon all with which it comes in contact. Society is corrupt through sin. The only thing that prevents utter demoralization is the, at times, almost unrecognized existence of God's church in the world. Abraham pleading for Sodom, and the divine promise not to destroy the city if only ten righteous can be found there will come to mind as an illustration of the principle (Genesis 18).

It is not difficult to see the quiet but powerful effect of a good man or woman upon any company. We have all noticed how conversation among a group of worldly people will receive a distinct check to profanity and impurity by the entrance into the group of a really good person. In the same way the moral tone of a whole household or business firm can be lifted by the unassuming goodness of one influential member.

Such unobtrusive power, however, requires a goodness that is an essential part of the character. Something merely put on outwardly, for purposes of convenience or selfish gain, will usually be quickly detected. True goodness is something that is *felt*—and so is hypocrisy.

Goodness is something that can quickly deteriorate, and its influence will not reach very far on merely past reputation. Men forget a passing miscarriage of a gift far more easily than they do a failure in character. Our Lord put it very bluntly, "Salt is good: but if the salt have lost its savor wherewith shall it be seasoned? It is neither good for the land nor for the dunghill; but men cast it out" (Luke 14:34,35).

To remain good, in the true sense of the word, means a close walking with the Spirit. But where such a daily walk is maintained, by divine grace, it is blessed to know that goodness will be a sure and certain reward as a fruit of the Spirit. Fellowship with all that is good will inevitably produce goodness, as truly as sunshine brings color to the peach and sweetness to the apple.

ACTIVE GOODNESS

Goodness is not only passive, however, as a quality of character. It has an active manifestation in the form of good works. "A good man, out of the good treasure of his heart, bringeth forth good things" (Matthew 12:35).

This statement, from the greatest of all teachers, is clear as crystal in its three stages of truth: First, the essentially good man; second, the resultant "treasure" which a man like that is bound to store up in his heart; third, the bringing out of good things before all. It was once my privilege to know intimately a man like that in Scotland, and it was delightsome of an evening to draw out by the art of conversation the "good treasure" stored in his heart. After many years I still feel the enrichment. The shallowness of some people's con-

54

versation is often an indication of the poverty of their goodness!

Let us be under no illusion where good works are concerned. A faith, or a presumed experience of the Spirit of God, that does not produce good works and good deeds is sheer vanity. "That they may *see* your good works, and glorify your Father which is in heaven." "That ye might walk worthy of the Lord unto all pleasing, being fruitful in every good work." "Be careful to maintain good works" (Matthew 5:16; Colossians 1:10; Titus 3:8).

Here is a fruit of the Spirit which all men see and value. Here is convincing proof, even to the unbeliever, of the reality of what Christ has done for our souls. "That they may by your good works, which they shall behold, glorify God in the day of visitation" (1 Peter 2:12). To pile up reference after reference is unnecessary.

It is worthwhile, though, to point out that those who boast of deep spirituality are sometimes most in danger of neglecting the more practical aspects of true religion. Nothing has pleased me more when in the great Pentecostal assembly in Stockholm, than to see the "Ark" they have moored in the river near by; where, night after night through the winter, they give free and comfortable lodging to scores of poor men, and provide meals for hundreds more. Such a "practical Pentecost" would indeed delight the heart of the apostle who was not afraid to tell masters who could "teach and admonish one another" that they must give to their "servants that which is just and equal"; or wives who could sing in "psalms and hymns and spiritual songs" that they should be exemplary in the practical side of home and family life (Colossians 3:16; 4:1). Such is the fruit of the Spirit which is goodness; and a scriptural corollary of being full of the Spirit is to be "full of goodness" (Romans 15:14).

THE THRONE OF RIGHTEOUSNESS

There is a deeper side to goodness than anything we have mentioned yet. Absolute goodness is nothing more nor less than moral perfection.

One of the grandest statements in the Bible is in Nahum 1:7: "The Lord is good, a stronghold in the day of trouble." It is just because He is good that He can be a stronghold. The moral government of the universe is established upon a throne of righteousness. It is only faith in this sure fact that can hold the soul steady in the storms of life. Without such a basic faith all would be chaos. No wonder we are continually told to "praise the Lord for His goodness" (Psalm 107).

The underlying gospel of the fruit of the Spirit is that men can become like God by walking with Him, and through the indwelling Spirit of His Son.

And the tremendously important fact for all who have received an experience of the Holy Spirit's fullness accompanied by unmistakable manifestations of His power, is that the fruit of the Spirit must become an essential accompaniment of that power as they go onward. If not, then they will end in spiritual bankruptcy after having been given the possibility of a fadeless crown. "Though I have the gift of prophecy, and understand all mysteries and all knowledge; and though I have all faith, so that I could remove mountains, and have not love,

. . . it profiteth me nothing" (1 Corinthians 13:2, 3, R.V.).

Goodness can be the consolation and reward of those who may never be conspicuous for brilliant gifts. Dorcas was no prophetess like Deborah, or even the daughters of Philip, but the fact of her having been "full of good works" has been recorded for the inspiration of Christian womanhood all down the ages (Acts 9:36). In Barnabas this particular fruit of the Spirit appeared in such prominence and richness that it is recorded of him: "For he was a *good* man, and full of the Holy Ghost and faith" (Acts 11:24).

May God give His church many more such pastors as the first one with whom the privileged assembly at Antioch was blessed.

8

Faithfulness

It is rather unfortunate that the Authorized Version of the English Bible a little obscures the significance of the seventh fruit of the Spirit by translating it "faith."

Faith, in any special sense, is not a fruit of the Spirit, but one of His gifts (1 Corinthians 12:9); and even the faith that saves a man is described as the "gift" of God (Ephesians 2:8).

The significance of the word in Galatians 5:22 is *faithfulness,* as it is rendered in the American Revised Version. Moffatt translates it "fidelity." A similar passage where the Authorized Version uses the word "faith," but where the obvious meaning is "faithfulness," is Romans 3:3, which Moffatt translates, "Is their faithlessness to cancel the faithfulness of God?" and which Newberry renders, "Shall their unfaithfulness make the faithfulness of God of none effect?"

The fruit of the Spirit we are now considering is therefore that fine quality of character known as faithfulness, trustworthiness, loyalty, reliability, constancy, or steadfastness.

A Bedrock—Natural and Spiritual

Even in the natural sphere, faithfulness is the bedrock on which society ultimately rests. All business transactions, all international treaties, all conjugal and family relationships are based upon an assumption of faith in the contracting parties. Their success or failure largely depends upon the faithfulness or unfaithfulness of those involved. Faithlessness brings confusion.

The truly fundamental nature of faithfulness is even more marked in the spiritual realm. All God's dealings with men, and all our personal hope of salvation in Christ, is founded upon the one supreme fact that "God is faithful" (1 Corinthians 1:9). Remove this, and all assurance vanishes. But with it, and resting upon His faithfulness, we can say, "I am persuaded that he is able to keep that which I have committed unto him."

The great covenants of Scripture all depend upon the faithfulness of the parties involved. In the Old Covenant God was faithful, but Israel, the other party, failed. The difference in the New Covenant is that our side is guaranteed by the faithfulness of Christ, who is the "Amen, the faithful and true witness"; and our "faithful high priest"; and "sanctifier." (Hebrews 8:9,10; Revelation 3:14; Hebrews 2:17; 1 Thessalonians 5:24).

It is important to base our understanding of the fruit of the Spirit upon these great, basic attributes of the Godhead, for the reason that the fruit we are considering is the direct result of our having been made "partakers of the divine nature" through the work of the Spirit in regeneration; and because it grows in our individual lives as we walk in fellowship with God by the Spirit.

It is thus that we come to share the divine quality of faithfulness, and obtain "mercy of the Lord to be faithful" (1 Corinthians 7:25). Natures that have no reliability in themselves can be transformed; and those naturally loyal can have their loyalties fixed to the highest ends.

I once heard my friend Howard Carter give a splendid illustration of this principle by likening our human natures in all their unreliability to the loose power of cement. But when water is mixed with the cement it turns it into concrete as hard as rock. So the living water of God's Holy Spirit can turn our lack of steadfastness into magnificent faithfulness, and convert many an impulsive "Simon" into a devoted "Peter."

NOTABLE EXAMPLES OF FAITHFULNESS

There are many examples of faithfulness in the Scriptures. Moses is described as being "faithful in all his house" (Hebrews 3:2), his faithfulness evidently consisting mainly in his obedience in making everything in the tabernacle "according to the pattern." Caleb and the seven thousand in the time of Elijah are also inspiring examples of faithfulness to God in times of apostasy (Numbers 14:24; 1 Kings 19:18).

In the New Testament, besides the chief apostles, there is special mention made of Epaphras, who is lovingly described as "a faithful minister of Christ." His faithfulness found one rare and fruitful expression by "laboring fervently" in prayer (Colossians 1:7; 4:12).

Young preachers should notice that Timothy was

commended for being "faithful in the Lord" (1 Corinthians 4:7), and his reward is found in those responsible duties assigned to him in the epistles that bear his name. All who aspire to positions of high leadership and responsibility must remember that faithfulness is a prime necessity.

Perhaps the most striking and beautiful instance of all is the story of Onesimus, the runaway slave, who became converted in Rome, and was then sent back to his master Philemon with an exquisite letter of recommendation from Paul. He is particularly described as a "faithful and beloved brother" (Colossians 4:9). He provides an outstanding example of *sand* becoming transformed into *rock* by the indwelling Spirit of Christ.

FIDELITY IN MINISTRY

Trustworthiness in ministers is of the first importance. "It is required in stewards that a man be found faithful" (1 Corinthians 4:2). We suggest three lines for special attention:

(a) *Faithfulness in Preaching*

"A true witness delivereth souls," and a preacher of the gospel must above all other things be faithful. In spite of incidental persecution at times, nothing will so certainly win respect in the long run.

Loyalty to the truth must equally mark all teaching; for newborn babes in Christ must have "the sincere (without fraud) milk of the Word." There are also times when faithfulness must cause us to "declare all the counsel of God" (Acts 20:27), and keep back none of the truth that God has taught us. We must be careful, though, not to confuse this with needless pushing of controversial questions on all occasions. Paul was referring to a period of three years of ministry at Ephesus, and not to a passing engagement. We are not obliged to bring out every one of our beliefs every time we preach.

(b) *Loyalty to Our Promises*

Perfidy is always obnoxious; but in a preacher it is enough to disqualify him for his office. A minister of Jesus Christ must be a man whose "word is his bond."

This should apply to every detail of his work—to the keeping of either preaching or visiting engagements, and to promises made to rich or poor, young or old alike. He will find it worthwhile to go to great expense, if need be, of time, money, leisure, or strength to keep a promise. Nothing will make a finer background for a man's influence as a preacher than a reputation for trustworthiness where his word is concerned.

(c) *Reliability in Business*

A man set apart for prayer and the ministry of the Word is wisest to follow the apostolic precedent, and leave all "serving of tables" to others. Business, in the ordinary sense of the word, is a sphere where a preacher of the gospel is not called to shine; some good preachers have made shipwreck of their ministry by forgetting this.

Nevertheless, there are certain items of business inseparably connected with church work with which a pastor has legitimately to become interested. And there is, of course, the regular business of his private affairs and household.

In all these things a minister of Christ should especially avoid real personal debts of any kind, and should, by every means in his power, build up a reputation among all who have any business dealings with him for the strictest integrity as to all money matters. His faithfulness and reliability among local tradesmen should be proverbial.

"Faithful Unto Death"

The comforting and inspiring principle that ultimate rewards for God's servants are going to be bestowed for faithfulness, and not for brilliance (Matthew 25:21), has been pointed out too many times to need enlarging upon here.

It should be remembered, however, that faithfulness implies diligence, as the parable is especially designed to teach. It is more than the mere faithfulness of the servant who gave back to his master all he had received, without loss; it is the faithfulness of diligent service.

Faithfulness, like all the other fruit of the Spirit, grows. It begins with quite small matters; indeed, if not manifested in small things it will never have opportunity in the greater (Luke 16:10). How very great those opportunities may be only eternity will reveal.

The rewards for faithfulness include as one of their chief and most alluring features enlarged service (Luke 19:17).

But this is not all. The glimpses given of the final award for faithfulness are enough to inspire every fainting mind, and ravish every loving heart. For those who are "*with Him*" in that bright glory are "the called, and chosen, and *faithful*" (Revelation 17:14). This will be the crowning reward for faithfulness and loyalty to Christ. And after all, it is fitting that those specially marked by faithfulness should compose those armies of heaven which should follow the King of kings and Lord of lords, upon whose banner will be displayed the word *"faithful and true"* (Revelation 19:11-14).

The fruit of His Spirit, gained by walking with Him steadfastly below, will then come to its harvest. "Be thou faithful unto death, and I will give thee a crown of life" (Revelation 2:10).

9

Meekness

Three things are outstanding with regard to meekness. It is a very rare quality of character. It is exceptionally precious in the sight of God. It is the most challenging feature in the teaching of Christ.

Not to Be Confused with Weakness

True meekness needs careful definition. In our English language we have another word that sounds much the same—"weakness." We are afraid a lot of people confuse not only the two words, but the two qualities of character. But, of course, the actual difference between meekness and weakness is immense. Real meekness requires great strength of character.

The most conspicuous Biblical illustration of a meek man is Moses. He was "very meek, above all the men which were upon the face of the earth" (Numbers 12:3). Yet he was one of the greatest leaders that history has produced. He could be stern enough when occasion demanded; as for instance, when he made the worshipers of the golden calf drink the dust of their own idol (Exodus 32:20). But that was holy zeal for the sake of Jehovah. When his own name was reproached by Aaron and Miriam, he did not make the slightest attempt at retaliation (Numbers 12). This reveals the true caliber of the man, and his meekness.

Stephen is another good example. His meekness shines in his prayer for his murderers (Acts 7:60); but there is no trace of weakness in his scathing indictment of the Sanhedrin—"Ye stiffnecked and uncircumcised in heart and ears, ye do always resist the Holy Ghost" (v. 51). One notices the same qualities as in Moses—zeal for God, but meekness as to self.

It is superfluous to mention the One who though "led as a lamb to the slaughter" yet cleansed the temple with a whip!

A CONDITION OF SPIRIT

Peter uses the very beautiful expression, "A meek and quiet spirit, which is in the sight of God of great price" (1 Peter 3:4). It is noteworthy that the New Testament usually speaks of a meekness of *spirit* (Galatians 6:1; 1 Corinthians 4:21).

It is in this respect that meekness differs from gentleness. In many ways these two fruits of the Spirit are the same; but meekness is an inward and passive thing, whereas gentleness is an outward and active thing. A man *feels* meek, but he *acts* gently.

Stephen's face was "like the face of an angel" (Acts 6:13) just because he *felt* like one. It was the meekness and serenity in the man's spirit shining out; doubtless he was unconscious of the manifestation himself. In the very nature of the case, meekness becomes spoiled by too much self-consciousness, though its inward blessings afford the deepest joy and peace. A truly meek spirit must be one of the hardest things on earth to imitate. *Gentleness* can sometimes be used when the spirit does not *feel* gentle; but if the heart is not really *meek* the inward fire of anger and pride will inevitably reveal itself sooner or later.

The Challenge of Christianity

The fact that Christ definitely taught meekness as an essential for all His disciples (and no one will dispute that He practices His own teaching to the end), makes one of the most challenging features of Christianity. One has only to look at the resurgence of intense nationalism now going on in nearly every part of Europe, with all it involves of pride and armament, to see how intensely difficult nominally "Christian" countries are finding it to harmonize their natural fevers of worldly vanity with the true spirit and teaching of Christ. A return to the old heathen deities of force, in preference to Christ, has been recommended by certain leaders. The embarrassing position of most of the churches in the event of war and the persecution of the "conscientious objector" all show how repugnant anything like an actual manifestation of the Spirit of Christ in meekness is to the man of this world. Compromises are futile; it is better to accept the challenge. Whether we personally fail or not, we had better admit that meekness is the only true Spirit of Christ and Christians; not only in case of war, but in business, and in all things— even in the Church.

When to Be Meek in the Church

There are certain specific matters in which Christians are very specially commanded to manifest a meek spirit in their assembly life. There is little hope of showing the world a victorious example of true meekness in big, outward issues, if we do not begin "in the family."

(a) *Restoring Backsliders* (*Galatians* 6:1)

Backsliders, if repentant, are to be *restored* "in a spirit of meekness," and their misdeeds forgotten, even as God forgets our forgiven sins. This warning is necessary because the pride of those who have not failed in the very way they have, would love to keep reminding them of their lapse. The reason for this—the consciousness of personal frailty on the part of those who sit to judge—should appeal to all men of sense. It is only the grace of God that has kept the judge from being the criminal!

Of course this does not abolish the rightful place of church discipline: it only indicates the spirit in which it must be used.

(b) *Answering Opponents* (1 *Peter* 3:15).

"Give an answer . . . with meekness." It is a splendid thing to be always ready with a convincing reply to the man who asks for it, but it must be given in a meek spirit. Our greatest spiritual blessings are no matter for self-boasting, but all of grace. We need to remember this with regard to Pentecostal blessings as much as any others.

To argue and strive in a contentious spirit, even for the most precious truths of our faith and hope, is likely to make the very spirit of our striving deny the truth of our testimony. We have all heard of that holiness convention where they got so hot discussing their differing doctrines of holiness that the only thing they effectually proved was that none of the disputants possessed it.

It is also worth remembering that even if brilliant argument compels a man to an intellectual agreement, his heart may only be, for that reason, all the more antagonized against the truth we wish him to receive, unless he has felt the meekness of our spirit also. To vanquish a foe is not the same as to convert him into a friend. Our immediate purpose as Christians is conversion, not conquest.

(c) *Receiving the Word* (*James* 1:21)

Listening to the Word is a great art—perhaps as great as preaching it. If our listeners prepared themselves by prayer as much as our preachers, what a revival we should enjoy! Human hearts are like soil, and their condition determines the result of the sowing far more than the skill of the sower.

Meekness ensures a condition of receptivity likely to yield a good harvest. This does not mean a foolish credulity that soaks in every new or strange doctrine. What it does mean is a laying down of all rebellion in spirit, and a readiness to obey at any cost what may be fairly proved to be the "sincere milk of the Word." It also implies a putting away of that foolish pride which refuses to admit that anything more can be learned upon the particular subject in hand.

(d) *"Meekness of Wisdom"* (*James* 3:13).

True wisdom is always marked by humility, and the "meekness of wisdom" expresses a delightful truism. Paul recommends it to Timothy (and surely through him to all young preachers, and old ones too!): he is to "instruct (correct) those that oppose themselves" (2 Timothy 2:25), with meekness. Especially with the older men and women (1 Timothy 5:1,2). Not lording over God's people, but humbly giving a calm reason for every suggestion and reproof, that must appeal to the spirit of Christ in every true believer.

The victories won by meekness in pastors and preachers, especially the younger, are worth far more than all the doubtful benefits of hastily standing on dignity and asserting the prerogatives of office. Probably nothing indicates a ripening of character in Christ more than an obviously meek spirit.

THE PROMISES TO THE MEEK

They are very many and very beautiful. "The meek shall eat and be satisfied" (Psalm 22:26). "The meek will He guide in judgment, and the meek will He teach His way" (Psalm 25:9). This is logical; it is easy to see that a meek spirit before God is in a much better position to receive divine guidance than a proud one.

The most famous promise of all is that made by our Lord, "The meek shall inherit the earth" (Matthew 5:5). The world scoffs at this; all human experience seems to point the other way, the meek get pushed out. Philosophy feels it ought to be so, but grapples with the problem in vain. Only faith triumphs, and cries, "It shall be done."

One day I watched a queue of people waiting to get in somewhere. A big husky fellow came along, and impudently pushed himself into the head of the line. But a policeman had seen it, and came along and made him go right down to the tail. Everybody looked pleased; our consciences bear witness with the truth, and we feel that is how it ought to be. Faith believes that as surely as God is still on the throne, it will happen like that one day, and the pushers will be made to take their right place. "The last shall be first, and the first shall be last."

While we wait for that day, our hearts embrace the most beautiful of the promises made to the meek by the only One who would dare to say to himself, "I am meek and lowly in heart." The reward of going with Christ through the school of meekness is that we *find rest to our souls* (Matthew 11:25). Such rest is in itself a sufficient and great reward. It is the first fruits of the harvest from the fruit of the Spirit which is meekness.

10

Self-control

The term "self-control" gives a much better understanding to readers of the English Bible of what is really intended by the last-named fruit of the Spirit than the word "temperance." Newberry gives it, and also the American Revised Version, in both Acts 24:25 and 2 Peter 1:6. "Temperance," for so many people, has special associations merely with strong drink; whereas the word in the Bible is intended to cover the whole range of human appetites, not only the physical, but the mental and spiritual, too.

The power to be "temperate in all things" is a great and important Christian virtue, and is a sure mark of growth in grace. Lest we imagine that the self-control under consideration is simply to be attained by purely natural self-discipline, it is well to emphasize at the outset that it is a fruit of the Spirit, and is the result of His help and grace, and the outworking of His life in the believer. Its possibilities are as much for those who have the very minimum of personal strength of character as for those whose wills are naturally forceful. Indeed, those with exceptionally strong natural willpower may be the very ones most in need of that sweet temperance which is a fruit of the Spirit.

THE CHRISTIAN ATHLETE

Paul has a great passage about this in 1 Corinthians 9:24-27: "Every man that striveth for the mastery is temperate in all things . . . I keep under my body, and bring it into subjection." The whole metaphor is taken from the old Grecian games in which every competitor had to undertake at least ten months' rigorous training before entry was allowed.

On this very liner on which I am traveling as I write there is a noted Finnish wrestler. Morning by morning, he is to be seen keeping himself in training by running and skipping and other exercises, and it is specially noteworthy that he will not touch either strong drink or tobacco, however much the other passengers tempt him to do so. His physical fitness is superb. The heat of the Equator made no difference to his exercise; he carried on just the same, though in a bath of perspiration.

And yet there are people who think it bordering fanaticism if a Christian takes as much pains to maintain the spiritual fitness of his soul. No wonder we have so few spiritual athletes. But God still has rewards for His Daniels (Daniel 1:8-21). Is there not just here the explanation of the scarcity of real *leaders* in the Church?

PHYSICAL SELF-CONTROL

This may be considered under two heads: things that are unlawful, and things that are lawful.

(a) *Unlawful Lusts*

Little need be written here about the necessity of self-control. Indeed it is not temperance that is needed, but total abstinence. All unbridled passion brings its own retribution; and with it the sense of deeper doom to follow. No wonder "Felix trembled" when Paul spoke to him about self-control. "Abstain from fleshly lusts, which war against the soul."

It should be solemnly remembered that nothing opens the door to downright demon possession so surely as continual self-indulgence in that which is physically unlawful.

(b) *That Which Is "Lawful."*

There is a large field for perfectly legitimate physical pleasure, and in this sphere we must be careful not to so misinterpret self-control that we cross the line into a misguided infliction of denial upon our bodies that is unnatural and repulsive to normal people, and may subject us to even fiercer temptations. It is not the Spirit of God, but seducing spirits, that forbid to marry and command to abstain from meats, etc. (1 Timothy 4:1-3). The passage is well worth pondering as a help to balance.

Nevertheless, even perfectly legitimate physical appetites must be kept firmly in hand. The exact attitude is splendidly stated in 1 Corinthians 6:12: "All things are lawful for me, but all things are not expedient: all things are lawful for me, but I will not be brought under the power of any." That is it! *not be brought under their power!* The body must be the servant, *never* the master.

74

The reasons for this careful and rigid self-control, even in lawful things, are various:

1. *Brotherly Love.* We have sympathetically to consider the effect of our own gratification upon a weaker character, that so far knows little of the Spirit's fruit of temperance, and may therefore be led by our example into personal sin. This is one of the most fundamental principles for the governing of all our actions as Christians. (Read Romans 14 for a detailed exposition of it.)

2. *Personal Victory Over Sin.* The body is the weakest point in our personal conflict with sin (Romans 6:12; 7:18), and therefore needs a reinforced guard at all times. Again and again the foe enters here, and sometimes temptation is successfully resisted in the spiritual sphere, only to be finally succumbed to in the physical. It is to be specially noted that experience and blessing on the line of spiritual gifts is no reason for abating intense watchfulness against the sins of the body, or resting in a hasty self-confidence. David had composed wonderful psalms under the anointing of the Spirit; but he committed adultery nevertheless when sudden temptation came in an indolent moment.

3. *Fitness for Service.* The condition of our body greatly influences our fitness for spiritual service. It is this principle that lies at the root of fasting. The condition of the body reacts inevitably upon the mind, let alone the spirit. We have all heard of, or experienced, the proverbial sleepiness of the average English Sunday afternoon congregation, after the proverbial English Sunday dinner. Spurgeon described it as "full of roast beef and un-

belief." In America the preacher is usually invited out to a tremendous supper about 6:30 p.m. and then expected to preach like an angel at 7:30! In Sweden it is the cup of coffee which seems almost indispensable for the inspiration of some preachers—and the good temper of their congregations!

Happy is the Christian who is free from bondage to all these things, though he may use them on occasion. Abstinence is usually the handmaid of true spirituality. This principle was at the root of the old Nazarite vow (Numbers 6); and was surely in the mind of our Lord when He said, "This kind can come forth by nothing but by prayer and fasting" (Mark 9:29). It is noteworthy that the Holy Spirit spoke in the assembly at Antioch "as they ministered to the Lord *and fasted*" (Acts 13:2).

It is easy to mock at physical self-denial; but if its rewards are increased spiritual power and increased sensitiveness to the voice of the Spirit, it is worth practicing.

MENTAL SELF-CONTROL

Those who would be shocked at the suggestion of personal physical licentiousness, may after all be guilty of gross intemperance on other lines—perhaps more serious.

Anger is a grievous and common form of intemperance of the soul. "He that is slow to anger is better than the mighty, and he that ruleth his spirit than he that taketh a city" (Proverbs 16:32). It should be remembered that giving way to a sulky temper day after day is just as intemperate as a violent exhibition of unjustifiable rage.

Allowing the tongue to run away with us is another form of intemperance; whether it be in sheer gossip, uncontrolled levity, or abused confidences. The scriptural remedy is decidedly robust! James uses the emphatic word "bridle," and gives the illustration of a bit in the mouth of a horse (James 1:26; 3:2). This is indeed self-control.

Inordinate love of praise is another weakness that can become an intemperance. All of us are helped by kindly and well-deserved words of appreciation. But some preachers have become such slaves to popular applause that they can scarcely preach except to a roaring accompaniment of "Hallelujahs," which are, as likely as not, a mere form of praise for the preacher, instead of to God. Given opportunity they will exceed all the bounds of propriety and consideration for others on the platform—or off it. There are occasions when long sermons and "outspoken" or daring utterances are sheer mental intemperance.

Spiritual Self-Control

This may be a surprising possibility to some; but it is highly important to recognize its essential place in Pentecostal experiences. "The spirits of the prophets are subject to the prophets" (1 Corinthians 14:32); and the gift of tongues is perfectly under the control of the one who uses it (v. 28).

Our own spirits are exteremely susceptible to deep feeling (thus, Jesus was "troubled" in spirit, and Paul was "stirred," John 11:33; Acts 17:16). We therefore have to maintain a rule over our own spirits in a special way at any time when feeling is being deeply stirred, and the circumstances are such that control is highly desirable. In private the necessity for such control may not be present, and then we can allow our spirits untrammeled liberty for self-expression "to ourselves and to God."

But in public meetings of the assembly, for instance, the love of Christ for other souls will cause us to consider the time, and the place, and the company, before we allow ourselves absolute liberty for the use even of our spiritual gifts. Watchfulness is very specially advisable at those times, in meetings when our spirits are most likely to become excited, as during powerful sermons, emotional prayers, or sentimental hymns; or when others are exercising spiritual gifts. To control our own spirits is not quenching the Holy Spirit; it is manifesting the fruit of the Spirit. It is of the utmost importance that all Spirit-filled believers should learn to know the difference between the emotional moving of their own spirits, and those occasions when the Lord himself truly wishes to use them for inspired utterances in the form of a revelation. Unless our own spirits possess the fruit of the Spirit, which is self-control, we may make disastrous exhibitions in public of sheer unbridled and unprofitable emotionalism.

INWARD STRENGTH

The Greek word for temperance means "to have inward strength." That is to say, our inward strength of will is greater than all the outward strength of temptation, desire, or excitement. This is perfect self-control.

Such a condition is indeed enviable. To teach self-control to a man or woman who has, by years of self-indulgence, lost all power of either physical, mental, or spiritual resistance seems little short of cruel mockery.

To such the message of the fruit of the Spirit is good news indeed. It means that Christ within us can accomplish what we can never hope to do in our own strength; and that a continuous walking with Him will change the weakest of us into His image until men will begin to see in us something of that superb self-control, and divine equipoise in every situation, that always marked the Son of man. The inward strength is not ours—it is *His*.